SQUADRONS!

No. 9

THE FORGOTTEN FIGHTERS

PHIL H. LISTEMANN

ISBN: 978-2918590-57-6

Copyright

© 2015 Philedition - Phil Listemann

Updated October 2019, November 2021

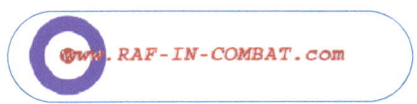

Colour profiles: Bill Dady/Claveworks graphics

All right reserved. No part of this book may be reproduced, stored in a retrieval system or transmitted in any form by any means, electronic, mechanical, photocopying, recording or otherwise, without prior permission of the author.

Glossary of Terms

Personel :

(AUS)/RAF: Australian serving in the RAF
(BEL)/RAF: Belgian serving in the RAF
(CAN)/RAF: Canadian serving in the RAF
(CZ)/RAF: Czechoslovak serving in the RAF
(NFL)/RAF: Newfoundlander serving in the RAF
(NL)/RAF: Dutch serving in the RAF
(NZ)/RAF: New Zealander serving in the RAF
(POL)/RAF: Pole serving in the RAF
(RHO)/RAF: Rhodesian serving in the RAF
(SA)/RAF: South African serving in the RAF
(US)/RAF - RCAF : American serving in the RAF or RCAF

Ranks

G/C : Group Captain
W/C : Wing Commander
S/L : Squadron Leader
F/L : Flight Lieutenant
F/O : Flying Officer
P/O : Pilot Officer
W/O : Warrant Officer
F/Sgt : Flight Sergeant
Sgt : Sergeant
Cpl : Corporal
LAC : Leading Aircraftman

Other

ATA: Air Transport Auxiliary
CO : Commander
DFC : Distinguished Flying Cross
DFM : Distinguished Flying Medal
DSO : Distinguished Service Order
Eva. : Evaded
ORB : Operational Record Book
OTU : Operational Training Unit
PoW : Prisoner of War
PAF: Polish Air Force
RAF : Royal Air Force
RAAF : Royal Australian Air Force
RCAF : Royal Canadian Air Force
RNZAF : Royal New Zealand Air Force
SAAF : South African Air Force
s/d: Shot down
Sqn : Squadron
† : Killed

Codenames - Offensive Operations - Fighter Command

Circus:
Bombers heavily escorted by fighters, the purpose being to bring enemy fighters into combat.

Ramrod:
Bombers escorted by fighters, the primary aim being to destroy a target.

Ranger:
Large formation freelance intrusion over enemy territory with aim of wearing down enemy fighters.

Rhubarb:
Freelance fighter sortie against targets of opportunity.

Rodeo:
A fighter sweep without bombers.

Sweep:
An offensive flight by fighters designed to draw up and clear the enemy from the sky.

THE BELL AIRACOBRA

When a replacement for the Curtiss P-36 was required in 1937, Curtiss responded by fitting an Allison in-line engine to the basic P-36 to produce the P-40. This combination had already been tried in the XP-37 which looked like a P-40 with the cockpit moved aft (a similar arrangement to the Dewoitine D 520. Two other manufacturers that submitted designs to USAAC specification X-609 were Lockheed, with the XP-38, and Bell, with the XP-39. Both were unconventional and raised eyebrows not only in Europe but also from within the USAAC.

The XP-39 was of conventional appearance in flight but, once the panels were removed, it proved to be totally at odds with normal fighter design. The engine was mounted behind the pilot to make room for the heaviest armament ever installed, at the time, in a single engine fighter – a 37mm cannon firing through the spinner via an extension shaft. A pair of 0.50-in machine guns was also mounted in the nose. This was a definite improvement on the standard US fighter machine gun only armament of the time and was a leap forward as the USAAC only just started to mount machines guns in the wings to complement the two nose-mounted weapons reminiscent of from the fighter aircraft of WW1.

Placing the engine over the centre of gravity would, it was thought, improve maneuverability while the cockpit offered a clear and extensive view. It was viewed with some alarm by some who envisaged a nose-tip as being the prelude to having the engine descend upon the unfortunate pilot. The other oddity for a single-seat fighter was the provision of a tricycle undercarriage. This was regarded with doubt by those who anticipated operating from improvised grass airfields but, surprisingly, it proved quite capable of flying from non-sealed strips. The engine also tended to remain where it should be (except in a major crash).

A prototype was ordered in October 1937 and flew on 6 April 1938. The first tests were encouraging. Various modifications took place to turn the aircraft into the XP-39B which showed a decrease in speed and rate of climb before it crashed. However, the USAAC had been impressed with the performance of the original version and, facing a lack of world-class fighters, gave Bell an order for thirteen YP-39s for service trials with Allison V-1710-37 engines. The first of these flew on 13 September 1940 with full armament and some armour protection for the pilot. Six of the thirteen were destroyed in accidents. A production contract was awarded for 80 aircraft in August 1939. These were to be P-45s but in the event the designation was changed to P-39C/D and soon named 'Airacobra'. The first twenty of them were P-39Cs, and had an Allison V-1710-35 engine, and were similar to the YP-39 but the next sixty were built as P¬39Ds with self-sealing tanks and four 0.30-in machine guns installed in the wings. Some armour was incorporated in the light of experience from operations in Europe. The first production aircraft flew in January 1941.

Early in the war, French and British purchasing commissions had been looking for aircraft from US sources and, of course, both countries showed an interest in the P-39 and this was soon followed by orders. The French Government requested 200 Airacobras in March 1940 with delivery to begin in October and, in April 1940, the Air Ministry ordered 675 in three separate contracts. The first 170 Airacobra Mk.Is were allotted serials **AH570 to AH739** (contract A-218) and the next 121, **AP264 to AP384**, then 84 with serials **BW100 to BW183** (contract A-1326 for the last two batches) and **BX135 to BX434** (contract A-1476) were allotted

P-39C DS173 taken shortly after its arrival in the UK in July 1941. The lack of wing guns can be seen here. The P-39C had been requested to test the 37 mm cannon.

to the final 300 to make the original order of 675. When the Lend-Lease Act was introduced in March 1941, the US requisitioned and orders were placed for the RAF: on 11 June 1941 for 150 P-39D-1 (41-28257/28406 with RAF serials **FA824-FA973**); then 344 more on 17 September (41-38220/41-38404, 41-38563 - 186 D-1s -, 41-38405/38562 - 158 D-2s with a 37 mm cannon replacing the 20mm - with RAF serials **FA974-FA999, FB100-FB417**) which included 144 earmarked for RCAF usage in Canada. Those Airacobras, equipped with a 20mm cannon and which should have received the denomination of Airacobra Mk.IA and IB for those with 37mm cannon, were never received by the RAF, due to the rejection of the type by that service, but were actually built for US or Russian needs instead. The Soviets received just over 100 under the Lend-Lease Act. However, as the 37 mm cannon was still a weapon banned for export, the Airacobras were to have a standard 20 mm cannon, two 0.50-in machine guns in the nose and four 0.30-in guns in the wings. The name 'Caribou' was selected but later abandoned.

The first Caribous came off the production line in April 1941. Prior to these arriving in the UK, three P-39Cs, 40-2981, 2983 and 2984, were shipped for trials, arrived in July 1941 and were allotted the serials **DS173**, **DS174** and **DS175**. DS173 was quickly assembled and first flew on 6 July 1941 before passing to A&AEE for handling trials. DS174 went to the Air Fighting Development Unit to test its aptitude for fighter operations while DS175 remained in reserve. These Airacobras were not standard as far as the RAF was concerned mainly due to the different armament and the 12-volt electrical system. The same month, deliveries of the production aircraft began but, when the USA entered the war, the Americans were prompted to seize some aircraft. These became P-400s as the British Airacobras, in turn, were not built under the USAAF standard. In all, the RAF took delivery of 241 Airacobra Mk.Is between September 1941 and March 1942. The balance was seized by the Americans or simply sent to the USSR when the fate of the Airacobra with the RAF was sealed at the end of 1941. In all, five of the first batch, 52 of the second, 77 of the third and all of the last were not delivered to the RAF.

AH573 was the first to be looked at and sent to AFDU as early as 30 July. Initial comments were not, however, very positive for the new RAF fighter. Critics immediately pointed towards the cockpit and the doors. The former was judged to be only suitable for small pilots while the latter was difficult to handle and enter and would be very difficult to exit in the even of a bail out. Other tests were conducted on AH574, which was tested for cooling, and AH590 carried out gunnery trials. Some modifications were suggested but the main complaint came from the 0.30-in guns as the recoil part could not be removed with the gun in position and the entire gun had to be removed for cleaning and maintenance after firing a complete ammunition load. There was no simple remedy for this. Each panel on the wing leading edge was fixed by 23 Phillips-head screws which required a special screwdriver and took about ten minutes to remove. This delayed the removal of the guns. For the 20 mm cannon, it was discovered that, to remove the breech-

Caribou/Airacobra AH621 taken during a test flight in the US before shipment to the UK. This aircraft was eventually handed over to the Soviets in November 1941.

block for cleaning, part of the radio installation and part of the instrument panel had to be removed. It was not practicable to remove this between flights so only lubrication was possible. It took two armourers 25 minutes to re-arm all guns. It took three hours and 45 minutes to remove and replace all guns (two hours for just the 20 mm cannon where an electrician and an instrument repairer were also required). Also, during actual firing, it was found that the 0.50-in guns fouled the windscreen badly and harmonization of the guns was difficult. For a day fighter, and in the environment the Fighter Command was operating in, the armament issues were seen as a major problem. Another Airacobra, AH701, came to the test flight fleet between January and September 1942 and was involved in gun heating trials in March 1942. AH701 was one of the last still flying for this purpose as AH589 had been sent back to the MU in June 1942 while AH590 was the victim of a minor accident on 24 December 1941. It was never repaired and was reduced to spares. Only AH574 had a long career with the RAF, being used for various tests until August 1947 when it was handed over to the Royal Navy.

At the same time DS173, with a 37 mm cannon, was tested for trials but, due to shortage of spares, they could not be completed. This aircraft had, in addition to the cannon, two 0.50-in and two 0.30-in mounted in the nose. Rounds carried were 15, 200 and 500 respectively per gun (it was normally 60, 1000 and 1000). There was no gun heating and the time for re-arming by two men was 20 minutes. The 37 mm was considered suitable for ground attack purposes but inadequate for air-to-air use. Maintenance complications made the aircraft unsuitable for general service use. Despite the findings of A&AEE it was decided to begin to equipping Fighter Command squadrons with the Airacobra for operational evaluation.

Airacobra AH574 seen while undertaking testing for the Royal Navy.
Note the underwing roundels that were not repainted after May 1942 when the new proportions were introduced. Left, the same aircraft in the scrapyard after the war.

This P-39D-1 (41-28360) was ordered under the Lend-Lease Act for the British and should have received the serial FA927. This P-39 was instead introduced in USAAF service and served as an advanced trainer Stateside.

August 1941 – March 1942

Victories - confirmed or probable claims: -

First operational sortie: 09.10.41
Last operational sortie: 11.10.41

Number of sorties: 8
Total aircraft written-off: 8
Aircraft lost on operations: -
Aircraft lost in accidents: 8

Squadron code letters:
UF

COMMANDING OFFICERS				
S/L Edward J. Gracie	RAF No. 29090	RAF	...	24.12.41
S/L Cyril A.T. Jones	RAF No. 43693	RAF	24.12.41	...

Squadron Usage

The first to be selected was No. 601 (County of London) Squadron at Matlask, one of the best Hurricane units of that time. Its CO was Squadron Leader Edward J. Gracie DFC who was a very experienced pilot with about a dozen claims to his tally. On 8 August 1941, one aircraft arrived at Coltishall and another at Duxford and eight pilots gained experience on type on the 10th in AH576, including the CO and F/L Jaroslav Himr and P/O Jiri Manak, the two Czech pilots of the squadron. On the 14th five more pilots made their first flight in AH577 while the squadron was continued to fly operationally on Hurricanes. On the 16th the squadron moved to Duxford to begin serious practice and in the evening more flights were carried out by the CO and P/O Manak. About 60 more flights were recorded by the end of August with the two already mentioned Airacobras supplemented by AH587 and AH588.

However, AH576 was written off on 29 August when Sgt George M. Briggs (RAAF) blacked out during aerobatics and suffered dizziness. He selected an incorrect undercarriage switch and the aircraft belly-landed and was declared beyond economical repair. On the 26th Cygnet G-AGBN (later ES915), apparently on loan from No. 51 OTU, arrived to provide practice with nose-wheel undercarriages. The three remaining Airacobras

> 'Jumbo' Gracie was a Battle of Britain veteran and had been leading 601 Sqn since August. He later served in Malta, where he continued to distinguished himself, but was posted missing in action during an intruder sortie on the night of 15/16 February 1944 in a Mosquito of 169 Sqn, a unit he had taken command of the previous October.

RAF pilots associated with the Airacobra are scarce but, among them, there were two Czech pilots, Jaroslav Himr (left) and Jiri Manak (right). Both would lead an RAF squadron later on. However, only one would survive the war. Jiri Manak was shot down on 28 August 1943 while leading 198 Sqn. He survived to be a PoW. Himr was killed in action on 24 February 1943 while commanding No. 313 (Czech) Squadron. *(Jiri Rajlich)*

used in August were supplemented by eight more in September and another ten in October. Close to 250 flights were recorded in September but, on 30 September, AH596 lost fuel pressure and force-landed six miles from Colchester. The pilot was slightly injured but the aircraft was written off. That incident came after AH583 had suffered, on 27 September, a drive-shaft failure and force-landed at Marham but returned to service. The transition seemed to be harder than intended!

Early in October the training was advanced enough to consider sending the Airacobra on operations. For this purpose, on 6 October, four aircraft left for detachment at Manston, for a test against the enemy, but bad weather prevented it. On the 9th F/L Himr in AH583 and Sgt Briggs in AH581 set off on a *Rhubarb* operation to Dunkerque, shooting up a number of personnel on a pier and a trawler. Next day, taking off from Manston, P/O Manak in AH595 attacked barges on a canal behind Dunkerque and returned to base safely after 45 minutes of flight. Twenty minutes later, S/L Gracie, in AH583, and Sgt Scott took off for a *Rhubarb* operation that was uneventful. On the 11th Himr (AH583), Manak (AH595) and P/O Chivers (AH584) went to Boulogne with a gaggle of Hurricanes but found no targets. The detachment returned to Duxford on the 12th. Although not known at the time, the Airacobra's RAF service had been completed! Despite this, the aircraft continued to give trouble. AH597 ended up in a ploughed field near Oakington due to faulty cockpit drill on 22 October but was repaired. By the end of the month, DS173 and DS174 were taken on squadron charge for further trials but only one flight for each was recorded in November and in all the Airacobra logged around 170 hours of flight time but at the cost of another Airacobra, AH603, which was wrecked on 21 November when the engine cut on take-off. The pilot, Sgt W.A. Land escaped injury. That month, on 8 November, the Under-Secretary of State for Air, Lord Sherwood, visited the station, bringing with him J.J. Winant, the American Ambassador. Later in the same day, five members of the Russian Mission inspected the Airacobras as the RAF was trying to find a way out for the dozens of Airacobras stored since the aircraft's rejection. Training continued in December at the same level despite many days where the weather prevented any flights. Accidents continued to occur. On 12 December AH601 force-landed due to fuel problems but its Canadian pilot, P/O W.R.P. Sewell, was not injured. However, the next day, P/O R.E.F. Sawyer (RAAF) was killed in AH581 when it suffered engine failure on approach to Debden. On the administrative side, F/L Jones was appointed OC of the Squadron on 24 December.

On 4 January 1942, the ground echelon of No. 601 moved to Acaster Malbis in Yorkshire but the aircraft were delayed by snow. All serviceable Airacobras flew up on the 6th. Firing trials at 27,000 feet showed that the cannon would fire 10 rounds and then freeze up. One of the 0.50-in machine guns refused to fire as the breech was iced up. That month the number of hours flown dropped to about 25 mainly due to the bad weather. On 10 February four aircraft, out of the six serviceable, were flown which the squadron recorded as an achievement. Acaster Malbis was a grass field that was often too soft for safe flying in winter. By now all concerned were becoming impatient with their temperamental mounts. On 13 February P/O McDonnell was killed when he spun into the bank of the River Ouse, near the airfield, in AH602. In all 601 logged about 120 hours in February. On the 23rd S/L Jones received a posting instruction to assume command of No. 79 Squadron flying Hurricanes and F/L Beake took temporary command of the squadron until the arrival of S/L Bisdee on 10 March. By that time, no more Airacobras had been added to the squadron strength. Indeed, on 1 March, only two aircraft were serviceable and, on the 8th, Fighter Command signaled that the squadron was to be re-equipped with Spitfire Mk.Vbs. The first of these arrived on the 10th with Bisdee. On 21 March a formation flight was carried out by P/O Pawon and Sgt Cleveland in AH592 and AH580 respectively and on the 7th 601 logged the last flight on the Airacobra when

Even though the Airacobra would eventually be rejected by the RAF, the aircraft was highly publicised and various media coverage organised. Here, we can see thirteen Airacobras of 601 Sqn lined up for a ceremony. In the foreground is AH595/UF-O which was not sent to the Soviets like many others but struck off charge in July 1942 and scrapped.

Three other photos taken from the same coverage. Top, the Airacobra chosen by Gracie, with the serial AH601 (not a coincidence!). Note that he didn't use an individual letter. AH601 was later lost in an accident in the following December.

A three-quarter front view of AH589/UF-L which was eventually passed on to the USAAF in January 1943.

Same event of the previous page but seen from behind. The other aircraft visible are AH602/UF-W and AH582/UF-N. Both would be lost in accidents while serving 601 Sqn.

Sgt Kohout took AH587 from Boscombe to Upper Heyford. By the 16th a full establishment of Spitfires was on hand and ATA pilots came to collect the Airacobras and take them to maintenance units.

The majority of the Airacobras delivered were packed and shipped to Russia. British records state 265 shipped with 54 being lost en route to the Soviet Union. They would be used mainly for ground attack sorties with considerable success. Others were diverted to the USAAC after Pearl Harbor as the P-400, as mentioned earlier, to differentiate them as having different equipment from USAAC-ordered aircraft. In all, 24 saw service with No. 601 Squadron and nine with research establishments which, actually, was a poor result. As a fighter, from the British point of view, the Airacobra was a failure.

For the Americans, the story would continue for a while and, of the British Airacobras stored in the UK, some aircraft missed the chance to be used by the Americans as one fighter group was originally scheduled to come to Britain. In the event, however, the 31st Pursuit Group was shipped over and equipped with Spitfires on arrival. Some Airacobras went to North Africa during Operation 'Torch' and continued to operate until 1944 on mainly ground attack and reconnaissance duties. For want of anything else available, Airacobras were used in the Pacific and stood up well to the climatic conditions. They were, of course, no match for the agile Japanese fighters, but that is another story.

Summary of the aircraft lost by accident - 601 Squadron

Date	Pilot	S/N	Origin	Serial	Code	Fate
28.08.41	Sgt George M. Briggs	Aus. 408000	RAAF	AH576		-
30.09.41	Sgt William A. Land	RAF No. 745528	RAF	AH596	UF-W	-
19.10.41	P/O Peter N. Hewitt	RAF No. 101025	RAF	AH582	UF-N	†
21.11.41	Sgt William A. Land	RAF No. 745528	RAF	AH603		-
12.12.41	P/O William R.P. Sewell	Can./ J.6290	RCAF	AH601	UF	-
13.12.41	Sgt Roy E.F. Sawyer	Aus. 403103	RAAF	AH581		†
07.02.42	Sgt Ernest G. Shea	Can./ R.79550	RCAF	AH585	UF-O	-
13.02.42	P/O Angus J. McDonnell	RAF No. 101020	RAF	AH602	UF-W	†

Total: 8

Summary of the aircraft lost by accident - Other units

Date	Pilot	S/N	Origin	Serial	Code	Unit	Fate
15.11.41	Cptm W.K.L. Handley	-	ATA	AH598		3.FPP	?
10.01.42	1st/O J. Mollison	-	ATA	AH696		1.FPP	-
14.01.42	1st/O J. Genovese	-	ATA (US)	AH693		16.FPP	-
28.01.41	no details available*	-	?	AH614		51 MU	?
07.05.42	no details available*	-	?	AP309		218 MU	?

*believed damaged in a ground accident and not repaired.

Total: 5

A colour photograph of the CO's Airacobra (AH601), while being re-armed, with the 601 emblem painted ahead of the door instead of the individual letter. For an aircraft not to wear an individual letter was against RAF regulations of the time.

With the RAAF

Many new aircraft types were introduced into RAAF service in 1942. This was done out of necessity and was not the result of deliberations as to what was the best aircraft for the job. With the rapid advance of the Japanese in early 1942 in Asia, and the fall of Singapore and the Netherland East Indies, Australia faced invasion. The threat was real and the Australian Government appealed to Great Britain and the USA for help. Both quickly responded and, as far as the USA was concerned, they offered, besides sending men and material, to deliver various aircraft types as a stop-gap measure.

The Americans planned to send two fighter groups, the 35th and the 8th, equipped with P-39/P-400 Airacobras for operational service in New Guinea. The aircraft were shipped to Australia and assembled at various places in the country. The Americans agreed to divert some of these fighters to the RAAF which was desperate for fighter aircraft. The first seven aircraft were P-39Fs in July 1942 (229 built). This type was very similar to the P-39D (554 built) which was itself very similar to the British Airacobra Mk.I/P-400. These first seven P-39s received the serial **A53-1 to 7**. In August the fleet was reinforced with seven P-39Ds (**A53-8 to 14**). Later in 1943 the RAAF took charge of more P-39s - four D models (**A53-15 to 18**) and one F in May 1943 (**A53-19**) and, eventually, one D (**A53-20**) and two Fs (**A53-21 & 22**) in July 1943. This brought the number of P-39s used by the RAAF to 22 but only sixteen were issued to squadrons. A P-400 (BW114) was also loaned for initial training at Laverton.

The Australians never planned use the Airacobra on operations except in case of emergency. They were received at a time when more modern and, more importantly, more suitable aircraft for the RAAF's needs were slow to arrive with the squadrons so the P-39s were spread out among various first line squadrons. The invasion never took place and in 1943, with the arrival of new and modern aircraft, the P-39s became useless and the survivors were all returned to the USAAF by November 1943. Often untold, and with a more discrete career compared to the much more publicised RAF Airacobras, the Australians actually flew more operational sorties than the British.

In all, four RAAF squadrons used the P-39 over the course of a year:

P-400 BW114 was the only Airacobra of British origin to have been used by the Australians (and that was only a loan). BW114 was part of the 100 P-400s repossessed by the Americans on 29 December 1941 and rushed to the Pacific after Pearl Harbor.

No. 23 Squadron, RAAF:
When war broke out this squadron was flying Ansons, but converted to Hudsons and CAC Wirraways in 1942, on maritime patrols. The threat from Japanese submarines was real as several had been sailing along the Australian coast and sinking coastal shipping. The squadron then left its base at Archerfield, Queensland, for Amberley (also in Queensland), where it began to receive P-39s at the end of August 1942. The unit was at that time under the command of Squadron Leader Keith McD. Hampshire. By the end of the year the squadron had eighteen Wirraways and six P-39s, A53-8 to A53-14, on strength. In other words, all of the second batch received by the RAAF. Flights began in September and consisted of formation, aerobatics, ground strafing and aerial combat. A total of 101 flights were carried out but serviceability remained low at 45%. However, some patrols were carried out by the P-39 that month with two on the 17th and three on the 25th. In October activity remained stable with 127 flights and much higher serviceability rate of 80%. This rate was maintained in November but with less flights, 82, completed. Several patrols were also carried during that period with eight in October and eleven in November. The activity dropped in December, only 42 flights, and two patrols were carried out on the 5th (the last ones for the squadron). Activity then increased to 109 flights in February and 16 in February . On the 26th all of the remaining P-39s (A53-11 having been damaged in an accident on 26th January) left the squadron and were taken on charge by   No. 83 Squadron the same day. Wing Commander Thomas R. Philp was, at that time, the OC, a posting he took in December 1942.

Keith Hampshire was a famous night fighter pilot who would later lead No. 456 (RAAF) Sqn in the UK and was awarded the DSO and DFC for his various actions. Before being sent to the UK, he served in Asia and Australia.

A53-9, T-Z, photographed in late 1942 while serving with 23 Sqn. If the upper surfaces had kept the US Olive Drab, the undersurfaces have been repainted in RAAF Sky Blue. The letter T was the squadron code letter. *(AHM of WA)*

Some of 23 Sqn's Airacobras lined up at Lowood late in 1942 with A53-13/T-Y and A53-9/T-Z visible. *(AHM of WA)*

No. 24 Squadron, RAAF:
Due to a lack of reliable documentation, little is known about the use of the Airacobra by this squadron. This unit had been engaged in combat against the Japanese, deploying to Rabaul with Wirraways, where it was decimated, before the survivors were evacuated to Australia. After the New Britain episode the squadron reformed at Townsville, Queensland, under the command of Squadron Leader John R. Perrin, and was equipped with various type of aircraft. Moving to Bankstown, New South Wales, it took charge of the first batch of seven P-39Fs the following month (A53-1 to 7). What is known is that they were used for patrols and possibly interceptions but there is nothing in the squadron's records so details are not known. From the movement cards and accident cards, it is known that A53-5 crashed on 26 October 1942 after an engine failure at Bankstown. The pilot, P/O Herbert C. Nette, was killed and the aircraft destroyed. Then A53-1 crashed on 19 February 1943 when the engine failed in flight. Pilot Officer Alan F. Tutt had to abandon the aircraft over South Luddenham, near Sydney. The same day, two Airacobras were scrambled at around 19.30 by fighter sector, following a possible raid, but it proved to be negative and both pilots, F/L Eric N. Faine in A53-3 and Sgt Frederick A. Hewlett in A53-6, returned to base safely. That led the squadron to mount patrols later on (P/O Wilfrid J. Pascoe in A53-2, Sgt Lex C. Dwyer in A53-7 and F/L Faine in A53-6), but nothing was reported. Five days later, it was the turn of A53-3 to have an engine failure at Bankstown, NSW, and was declared damaged beyond repair but its pilot, Sgt Desmond H. Harrison, was uninjured. By March only three P-39s were still in flying condition, a fourth having been damaged in an accident and had left the squadron. On 7 March another scramble took place (P/O Pascoe in A53-2), then another on the 26th (A.T. Tutt and Sgt Allan). All aircraft had nothing to report on return. In May two scrambles took place, one on the 6th with one Airacobra and another on the 16th with two aircraft, to identify aircraft but in both cases the aircraft proved to be friendly. Flights seemed to have continued until early June 1943 when the remaining P-39s were handed over to No. 82 Squadron.

Summary of the aircraft lost by accident - 24 Squadron

Date	Pilot	S/N	Origin	Serial	Code	Fate
26.10.42	P/O Herbert C. **Nette**	Aus. 400728	RAAF	**A53-5**		†
19.02.43	P/O Alan F. **Tutt**	Aus. 400108	RAAF	**A53-1**		-
24.02.43	Sgt Desmond H. **Harrison**	Aus. 405734	RAAF	**A53-3**		-

Total: 3

No. 82 Squadron, RAAF:

No. 82 Squadron was formed at Bankstown, New South Wales, on 18 June 1943. The unit was placed under the command of Squadron Leader Stanley W. Galton. The unit was to be equipped with P-40 Kittyhawks but, because of an initial shortage of this aircraft, one flight was consequently equipped with the P-39 Airacobra. The first Airacobras arrived three days later, coming from 24 Squadron, also based at Bankstown. By the end of June the following P-39s were on strength or scheduled to be delivered to the squadron: A53-2, 4 and 6 from No. 24 and A53-7, 10, 12, 13 (arrived in July), 14 and 19 (arrived in July).

Training commenced at once on both types and by 30 June the pilots had flown 39.2 hours on P-39s. The Kittyhawk flight flew thirty hours in the same time. Training was initiated at once with interception practice on both types, especially as the P-39's tricycle undercarriage was new for many pilots, because the squadron was in charge of the defence of the area and had to respond and carry out interceptions when necessary. On 22 June F/Sgt Reginald R. Bladwell in A53-12 and F/Sgt Frederick A. Hewlett (formelly 24 Sqn) in A53-6 took off for a practiced interception that was uneventful. The next day F/O Alan F. Tutt(formeley 24 Sqn) in A53-6 and F/Sgt Bladwell in A53-12 took off on a scramble that was also uneventful. Two more interceptions were flown on 24 June (F/O Robert N. Blenkhorn and F/O Tutt) and 28 June (P/O Keith E. Spargo and Sgt Richard C. O'Neill) with nothing to report on return to base. In July the Airacobra flight flew about 75 hours against almost 100 for the Kittyhawk flight. However the month started in the wrong way for the P-39s when A53-12 was badly damaged on the first day of the month. Flying Officer Reginald C. Barlow and F/O Spargo had taken off on a scramble but Barlow was injured when he had to crash-land his aircraft on return. The P-39 was not repaired and allotted for conversion and eventually returned to the Fifth Air Force in its damaged condition. In July scrambles and interceptions continued and the Kittyhawk began to be used for these also. In all, 32 scrambles or interceptions were carried out in July by Airacobras. Each time there was nothing to report. In August, the Airacobra fleet flew more than the Kittyhawks (100 hours against 67) but the Airacobra had been relegated to a training role with the last operational flight being recorded on the 6th when W/O Ronald .E. McGillivray scrambled at 2000 in A53-13. He returned to base one hour later with nothing to report. In September the Kittyhawk overtook the Airacobra with only thirty hours being flown by the Airacobras against 85 for the Kittyhawks. In the last days two accident occurred, on 30 August,F/Sgt Hewlett made a forced landing following an engine failure (A53-6) and on 2 September A53-7 did so too for the same reason (W/O McGillivray); in both cases the P-39s were declared repairable, but it is doubtful that they did before to be issued to the 5th Air Force The Airacobra was eventually withdrawn from the squadron before the month was over and the last flight was recorded on the 25th when F/O Tutt flew a local test.

Summary of the aircraft lost by accident - 82 Squadron

Date	Pilot	S/N	Origin	Serial	Code	Fate
01.07.43	F/O Reginald C. **Barlow**	Aus. 403998	RAAF	**A53-12**		-

Total: 1

A53-6/FA-F was the victim of an engine failure on 30 August 1943 but was declared repairable. The repairs seem to have never happened while in Australian service and it was probably delivered to the Fifth Air Force in its damaged condition. *(AHM of WA)*

No. 83 Squadron, RAAF:

No. 83 Squadron was formed in February 1943. The main purpose of the squadron was the interception of unidentified and hostile aircraft, surface vessels and submarines from Strathpine in Queensland. Its OC was Squadron Leader William J. Meehan but he was soon replaced by Squadron Leader Colin W. Lindeman the following month. Intended to be a CAC Boomerang unit, the squadron was allocated a couple of Airacobras on formation due to the lack of available Boomerangs. Most of the Airacobras were released from No. 23 Squadron. The first received was A53-8, which left the following month following a minor accident, and was soon followed by A53-9, A53-10, A53-12, A53-13, A53-14. Alongside the training on the type, defensive patrols and some interceptions of unidentified aircraft were regularly carried out in the Brisbane area (about 35 in February and March 1943 alone). The first patrol was flown on 26 February by F/Sgt James G. Stewart in A53-10 while the first interception of an unidentified aircraft took place on 16 March by F/L Sydney J. Richardson in A53-10. The first Boomerang arrived at the squadron in early April but the unit continued to carry out its operational flights, interception of unidentified aircraft, with the Airacobra. Twenty such flights were recorded on the American aircraft against a single on the Boomerang. This proved to be a false start as all of the Boomerangs and personnel were allocated to No. 85 Squadron on 25 April. In May close to thirty operational flights were recorded but, on the 11th, A53-9 was badly damaged in a flying accident and sent away (Sgt Arthur M. Walker, uninjured). It was never repaired and was eventually returned in its damaged state to the Fifth Air Force in August. In June, after this false start in April, the squadron began to receive more personnel and Boomerangs while forty more interceptions were carried out that month. The conversion continued in July and, from the middle of that month, the squadron became fully operational on the Boomerang. The last interception flown by an Airacobra was on the 14th when F/Sgt Lex C. Dwyer took A53-13 aloft. The squadron flew fourteen operational flights with the Airacobras that month and the remaining aircraft, A53-10 and 13, were handed over to No. 82 Squadron. The squadron flew bout 100 operational flights with the Airacobra.

P-39F 41-7141 seen while serving with the 35th FG at Strathpine circa 1942. This P-39 later became A53-7 in the RAAF and eventually served with 83 Sqn.
(AHM of WA)

SIMPLIFIED REGISTER

RAAF	US serial	Type	Unit	From	To	RAAF	US serial	Type	Unit	From	To
A53-1	41-7117	P-39F-1-BE	24 Sqn	7-42	2-43	A53-11	41-6805	P-39D-1-BE	23 Sqn	8-42	7-42
A53-2	41-7134	P-39F-1-BE	24 Sqn	7-42	1-43	A53-12	41-6944	P-39D-1-BE	23 Sqn	8-42	2-43
			82 Sqn	7-43	10-43				83 Sqn	2-43	4-43
A53-3	41-7157	P-39F-1-BE	24 Sqn	7-42	2-43				24 Sqn	4-43	6-43
A53-4	41-7163	P-39F-1-BE	24 Sqn	7-42	10-42				82 Sqn	6-43	9-43
			82 Sqn	6-43	10-43	A53-13	41-7085	P-39D-1-BE	23 Sqn	8-42	2-43
A53-5	41-7164	P-39F-1-BE	24 Sqn	7-42	10-42				83 Sqn	2-43	7-43
A53-6	41-7168	P-39F-1-BE	24 Sqn	7-42	9-42				82 Sqn	7-43	9-43
			82 Sqn	6-43	8-43	A53-14	41-6968	P-39D-1-BE	23 Sqn	8-42	2-43
A53-7	41-7141	P-39F-1-BE	24 Sqn	8-43	10-43				83 Sqn	2-43	7-43
			83 Sqn	6-43	7-43				82 Sqn	7-43	9-43
			82 Sqn	7-43	9-43	A53-15	41-6723	P-39D-1-BE	-		
A53-8	40-3017	P-39D-BE	23 Sqn	4-42	2-43	A53-16	41-6738	P-39D-1-BE	-		
			83 Sqn	2-43	4-43	A53-17	41-6929	P-39D-1-BE	-		
A53-9	40-3035	P-39D-BE	23 Sqn	2-42	2-43	A53-18	41-6947	P-39D-1-BE	-		
			83 Sqn	2-43	5-43	A53-19	41-7189	P-39F-1-BE	82 Sqn	7-43	10-43
A53-10	41-6758	P-39D-1-BE	23 Sqn	8-42	2-43	A53-20	41-6838	P-39D-1-BE	-		
			83 Sqn	2-43	7-43	A53-21	41-7235	P-39F-1-BE	-		
			82 Sqn	7-43	9-43	A53-22	41-7199	P-39F-1-BE	-		

Two Airacobras seen while stored. Left, A53-1 at No. 2 Aircraft Depot at Bankstown in 1942 and, below, A53-20 at No. 3 Aircraft Depot at Amberley in 1943. A53-20 was never used by the RAAF.
(AHM of WA)

The Bell Airacomet

The Bell P-59 Airacomet was the first jet fighter introduced to the USAAF inventory and was also the first American jet to fly when it first flew on 2 October 1942. Although thirteen service-test YP-59As and 100 production P-59As were ordered, the unsatisfactory performance of the design, due largely to the low power of the two General Electric gas turbine engines, led to the cancellation of the last fifty aircraft while the first fifty were delivered as twenty P-59As and 30 P-59Bs. The Airacomet was never used on operations and most served with the 412th FG, a jet advanced-training unit specially dedicated to operate the Airacomet, while the others went to USAAF or USN test establishments.

One YP-59 Airacomet, 42-108773, the third pre-production aircraft, was exchanged with the first production Gloster Meteor EE210. This aircraft, delivered on 27 June 1943, was retained at the factory for British use before being shipped to the UK. Upon its arrival in the UK on 9 September 1943, the Airacomet became **RJ362/G**. The 'G' indicated that a guard had to be placed on the aircraft when it was on the ground away from Farnborough where the RAE (Royal Aircraft Establishment) was stationed.

RJ362/G made its first flight at Gloster's Moreton Valence airfield on 28 October and delivered to the RAE eight days later where it made twenty flights with the Engine Research Flight (later re-named T Flight) between December 1943 and April 1944. Two sets of tests were run. Thirteen flights were performed before the engines were removed (having added ten hours to their run time), stripped and inspected by Power Jets Ltd. The engines were reinstalled in the aircraft for the second round of testing but these were cut short, after 6.5 hours, when the port engine deteriorated. The engine returned to Power Jets for another strip and inspection. In September 1944 the Airacomet was transported to Rolls Royce with the intention of installing Derwent engines for comparative trials. Although the installation was largely completed the aircraft was never flown in this form and it was later returned to the USA but did not fly again before being sold for scrap in June 1945.

Two photos of the Airacomet RJ362/G showing both sides.

The Bell Kingcobra

The Bell P-63 Kingcobra was the logical development of the P-39 Airacobra. The prototype XP-63 made its first flight on 7 December 1942. This aircraft was built mainly for export and the Soviet Union received the bulk of the production. The French and the Americans also used the aircraft with the latter only employing it in a training role Stateside.

Disappointed with the P-39, the British did not ask for any Kingcobras for their fighter force, nor did any of the other Dominions. However, the USA and the United Kingdom regularly exchanged aircraft for various research projects. Three examples were allocated to the UK for drag research at the Royal Aircraft Establishment (RAE) at Farnborough. **FR407** (P-63A-6-BE 42-68936) and **FR408** (P-63A-6-BE 42-68937) were first allocated and accepted by the AAF on 23 and 18 February respectively. Only FR408 was shipped to the UK, leaving the USA on 22 March 1944, while 42-68936 never became FR407 and remained Stateside as a trainer instead. FR408 was delivered to the RAE on 17 May but crashed at Farnborough on 31 July after the undercarriage failed to lower (S/L J.C. Nelson). It was declared damaged beyond economical repair and was struck off charge after only five hours and fifteen minutes in the air. It was replaced by **FZ440** (P-63A-9-BE 42-69423). Accepted on 15 July by the AAF, FZ440 was shipped to the UK on 2 August and arrived in UK on the 17th before being delivered to the RAE on 20 September. FZ440 was used by the RAE for various tests until the end of June 1948 and was sold for scrap in March 1949.

Summary of the aircraft lost by accident - RAE

Date	Pilot	S/N	Origin	Serial	Code	Fate
31.07.44	S/L John C. **Nelson**	RAF No. 58775	RAF	**FR408**	-	-

Total: 1

Kingcobra FZ440 replaced FR408 when the latter was lost in a flying accident. It remained in natural metal finish for its entire career with the RAE.
Below, some equipment installed on FZ440 to evaluate the practicability of the laminar flow wing in service. Note the upper wing roundel has been erased.

Two photos of Kingcobra FR408. Above, in the US before being shipped to the UK and having an "X" painted on the nose for experimental identification. Normally, when painted on the nose, the same "X" was also painted on the upper right wing panel (no US star in 1944) but it is doubtful that, for FR408, this 'X' has been painted on.
Below, FR408, seen after its arrival in UK, with the "X" painted over. It was officially struck off charge on 18 October 1945 due to a lack of spares. It became a spares source for FZ440 instead.

The Grumman Goblin

The Grumman Goblin was actually the export version of the Grumman FF-1, a two-seat fighter biplane ordered by the USN in the mid-thirties. This version was called GG-1 by the manufacturer and one was built as company demonstrator. In November 1936 the GG-1 was modified and sold to Canadian Car & Foundry (CC&F) as G-23. This company had decided to open an assembly plant line for the manufacture of aircraft and obtained, at the same time, a licence to produce the export variant of the FF-1/SF-1. The SF-1 was the scout version of the FF.

Despite commercial efforts, sales did not follow as expected and the first real chance to sell the G-23 in quantity came from Spain as it was now facing a bloody civil war. The Spanish Republican Government was interested in purchasing the first forty copies but soon added ten more G-23s. Due to the embargo on sales to Spain, the order was placed with the help of Turkey. Eventually, 34 of the fifty reached their destination between May and April 1938 where they would equip two squadrons. However, in the meantime, the Canadian Government realised what was going on and the true destination of these aircraft. The last sixteen aircraft were loaded and ready to be shipped out when the Canadian Government decided to step in. The sixteen airframes were disembarked and temporarily stored on the dock at Saint John (New Brunswick). The story of the Goblin in RCAF service started at that point. CC&F tried to sell the aircraft to the RCAF but it was already totally obsolete from the RCAF's point of view. This attitude changed abruptly when war broke out in Europe and the decision of the Canadian Government to enter the war on 6 September 1939. At that time the RCAF was about to embark on a massive expansion but was short of aircraft of all kinds and fighters in particular. The RCAF decided, with no great enthusiasm, to acquire the fifteen remaining aircraft (one had been sent to Mexico in October 1939). The time taken to fix all of the details, including the delivery of the airframes with Canadian specifications (which included three of them with dual controls), led to the delivery of these aircraft in October 1940. They were to equip a single fighter unit. They received the serials **334 to 348** in the RCAF nomenclature and were given the nickname of Goblin.

The unit selected was No. 118 (Fighter) Squadron which was reformed officially in December at Rockcliffe (Ottawa). The previous year the RCAF had intended for No. 115 (F) Squadron to take on the Goblin but the delays had obliged a change of plans. Flight Lieutenant Eric W. Beardmore took command of 118 Squadron. The fifteen Goblins were delivered in one shot and training commenced at once but soon problems arose because the aircraft were found to be in very bad shape and were grounded. This was due to the time the airframes had spent stored outside. The consequence for the squadron was that, if operational status was to be achieved within six months, all of the aircraft needed an overhaul. The first overhauled Goblin returned to the squadron on 1 May 1941. The squadron was now under the command of W/C Ernie A. McNab. By the end of the month five were on strength and in June all of the Goblins were back on strength. Intensive training was undertaken and, early in July, the squadron reached its operational readiness and was ready to move to its war station of Dartmouth in Nova Scotia where a new CO, the marvellously named (and Battle of Britain veteran) S/L Hartland de Montarville Molson took command. From that point 118 Squadron acted as a normal fighter squadron despite the low serviceability of the Goblins (about five to seven aircraft being available daily). That did not prevent losses, however, as one accident occurred on 23 July at Lawrence Lake. The pilot, Sgt Robert M. Bryant of Toronto, was killed. The aircraft flew into power lines and crashed while practicing low level attacks. There were two other accidents that summer. Goblin 346, on 29 July, suffered an engine failure and the pilot, P/O Clifford G. Pennock, hit trees while attempting a forced landing. He escaped injury. This pilot was later sent overseas and was killed in March 1944 while serving with No. 403 (RCAF) Squadron in England. The second accident occurred on 5 August (345) when the aircraft overturned after the landing gear collapsed on touch down. The pilot, F/L Arthur McL. Yuile also avoided injury. He was also a former Battle of Britain veteran with No. 1 Squadron, RCAF and was shot down twice and would resign his commission in September 1944. Both aircraft were declared repairable but as spares were difficult to obtain, and with the withdrawal of the type imminent repairs were not undertaken. Both Goblins were struck off charge in September and were converted to components.

In the following weeks the squadron began to prepare to receive Curtiss Kittyhawks. This was achieved in December. The career of the Goblin was not over, however, and some extra time was given to some of the surviving aircraft. Indeed, five were transferred to the School of Army Cooperation at Rockcliffe in December 1940 and this unit was re-designated No. 123 (Army Cooperation Training) on 14 January 1942 and placed under the authority of S/L W.W.S. Ross. It was given the role of familiarising the Army in working with aircraft. The Goblins were used as dive-bombers. This idea was short-lived, however, as the Goblin was found dangerous for this role

When he took command of 118 Sqn, Hartland de Montarville Molson, whose family owned Canada's largest brewery, was a Battle of Britain veteran, having fought with No. 1 Squadron RCAF on Hurricanes. He claimed one He111 destroyed and damaged three other aircraft. He returned to Canada but was never sent overseas again before leaving the RCAF in 1945 as a Group Captain. He continued the family business and became involved in politics.
(via Hugh Halliday)

and, due to lack of winter equipment for the engine and airframe, the number of flights remained low. When, on 3 February, a pilot was almost overcome by carbon monoxide, a recurring problem with the Goblin and never totally solved, made a forced landing and was hospitalised, the five Goblins were immediately grounded. The Goblins were stored until the following April when all of the airframes were broken up and the engines given to the Army. Since new and after overhaul, the highest time airframe was a mere 164 hours!

Summary of the aircraft lost by accident - 118 Squadron, RCAF

Date	Pilot	S/N	Origin	Serial	Code	Fate
23.07.41	Sgt Robert M. Bryant	Can./ R.65736	RCAF	336	-	†
29.07.41	P/O Cliford G. Pennock	Can./ J.5128	RCAF	346	-	-
05.08.41	F/L Arthur McL. Yuile	Can/ C.1328	RCAF	345	-	-

Total: 3

A well-known photo showing six Goblin in flight. The Goblins carried out about 120 scrambles during the second half of 1941. The Goblins flying are 341/RE-N, 335/RE-Y, 344/RE-W, 338/RE-M, 347/RE-V and 334/RE-A.

THE LOCKHEED LIGHTNING

The Lockheed Model 322 Lightning was a long-range twin-engine fighter with the pilot in a central nacelle and the tailplane carried on twin booms extending from the rear of the engine nacelles. It was designed for USAAC needs. Although the design had been ordered in small numbers by the USAAC as the P-38, the first large order came from the Anglo-French Purchasing Commission which placed a Letter of Intent to order 800 aircraft in April 1940. In practice the order was broken down into 667 complete aircraft with the balance being the value of spare parts. The intention was for the RAF to take 250 aircraft and the French to receive the remaining 417 that would be shipped to Casablanca for assembly and testing away from the risk of German air attack. With the fall of France the entire A-242 contract was assumed by the British. However, this contract was soon amended to provide for the delivery of two marks - 143 Lightning Mk.Is (serials **AE978-AE999** & **AF100-AF220**), with the original Allison V-1710-C15 engines, and 524 Lightning Mk.IIs (serials **AF221-AF744**) with the supercharged V-1710-F5L/F5R powerplants boosting top speed to 415 mph at 20,000 ft. Actually, only three were shipped to the UK, for service test purposes, (AF105, AF106 and AF107) arriving in March 1942 respectively to Cunliffe-Owen at Southampton for examination and experiment, A&AEE at Boscombe Down for flight evaluation and Royal Aircraft Establishment (RAE) at Farnborough for experiments and evaluation. Basically, the Lightning Mk.I was a P-38E without the superchargers and with the two propellers rotating in the same direction (against the advice of Lockheed). Tests of AF106 were limited due to a speed restriction on the Lightning I of 300 mph as there had been a number of accidents above that speed. It is important to note that the standard armament of one 20mm cannon and four 0.5-in machine guns was not fitted. The aircraft was found to be quite pleasant to fly but not very maneuverable for a fighter. Flying on one engine proved to be easy and the aircraft was still able to climb. On the other hand, the aircraft was found to be potentially dangerous for the pilot, in the case of a scramble with the engines running, because of the access to the cockpit by stepladder. However, the cockpit was found comfortable, well ventilated and rather well sound-proofed.

Two reasons led the RAF to reject the Lightning as a combat aircraft. First the poor performance of this 'export version' and, secondly, the fact that the USA had already seized a number of the aircraft built for their own use after their entry into the war in December 1941. Consequently, no more Lightnings were delivered to the British and the three aircraft were eventually handed over to the USAAF on 1 July 1943 (AF105), 10 July 1943 (AF106) and 2 December 1942 (AF107). The lack of superchargers was definitely the handicap that plagued the Lightning's performance and so sealed its fate with the RAF. The Mk.II had superchargers and, consequently, better performance and, if tested by the RAF, may have stood a chance of being introduced into service (possibly as a replacement for the Westland Whirlwind which, ultimately, had no similar successor). The P-38 Lightning gave very good results in the fighter-bomber role for the US Ninth Air Force, the counterpart of the RAF's 2 TAF and, in British hands, the Lightning could have done the same and maybe lives could have been saved. Indeed, the Whirlwind was replaced by the Hawker Typhoon, which became the main ground attack fighter of 2 TAF, a single engine aircraft that sustained heavy losses to ground fire. Many Lightnings were able to return home from Normandy on a single engine during the critical weeks of the summer of 1944.

All of the remaining 140 Lightning Mk.Is were taken on charge by the Americans and used as trainers after having been sent to the modification centre at Dallas. The first 20 retained their original V-1710-C15 (V1710-33) engines while the other 120 were re-equipped with V-1710-27/29s but without turbochargers. They became P-322s, a Lockheed designation, in the USAAF inventory. Only one Lightning Mk.II was completed (AF221). The other aircraft were delivered as P-38F-13, F-15, G-13 or G-15.

However, the Lightning chapter was not over as, later, two USAAF P-38s were used by the RAF in England in trials of the 'Master Bomber' role (directing attacks by Lancasters of Bomber Command). The first was a P-38J (44-23527) obtained from the USAAF in March 1944 by the CO of RAF Coningsby. Its nose was modified with a position for a bomb-aimer/observer and it received short-range communication radios to enable communication with the bombers. Coded '"DPA", no RAF serial was allocated as the transfer was unofficial. It was returned to the USAAF in November 1948 via the Netherlands. The second aircraft, a P-38L (44-24360), was used for a very short time, in August 1944, but was never modified.

Lightning Mk.I AE979 seen during a test flight. No armament was fitted. The other issue the RAF Lightning had to face was the fact that both propellers turned in the same direction (unlike the American P-38s). That was not seen as being a major issue in flight, and indeed it is not, but requires attention on take off. However, having two engines and propellers complicated maintenance and an aircraft could be easily grounded for lack of the right spare. The choice of identical engine/propeller units was also an economical consideration.

The Story of the Lightning 'DPA'

By 1944 No 5 Group had, in some respects, become a semi-autonomous formation within Bomber Command, having for example, its own target marking force separate to the Pathfinders and responsible to the 5 Group HQ. On of the Group's bases was No 54 Base which formed on January 1 1944 controlling Coningsby, Metheringham and Woodhall Spa and by mid 1944 the Base was commanded by Air Cdre Sharp. He had previously served as a liaison officer with HQ of the US 8th Air Force and when he left to assume his new position was 'lent' a P-47 Thunderbolt for his personal use. The heft fighter was not, however, to his liking and so it was exchanged of a Lockheed P-38 J Lightning, the twin boomed long range fighter being much more acceptable, and 44-23517 arrived in mid summer. At this time Bomber Command was heavily engaged in tactical support to the fighting in Normandy and No 54 Base Lancasters were flying regular daylight raids into France. Air Cdre Sharp's personal P-38 was flown on several of these raids during the first week of August by Sqn Ldr Owen, though whether as a target marker or an 'integral' escort is uncertain. On August 6 a second P-38, 44-24360, arrived at Coningsby for a series of trials. Referred to as the 'PB-38', it had a 'droop snoot' glazed nose to house a Norden bomb-sight and bomb aimer and had provision for two long range overload fuel tanks under the centre section. For security reasons it apparently carried no serials, but retained USAAF markings. Owen flew the 'PB' on a number of unspecified trials, whilst it was flown on at least one operation, a daylight raid on Deelen by 94 bombers on the 15th, by the irrepressible W/C Guy Gibson VC who was then acting as the Base Air Staff Officer.

The 'PB-38' was returned to the USAAF by the end of the month, but had left its mark on the staff at Coningsby, who took 'their' P-38 to Langford Lodge where it was modified as a two-seater with a glazed nose. Additionally, by the time it was collected in mid-September 44-23517 had also been fitted with an advanced suite of navigation aids, Loran and Gee, as well as twin VHF radio sets. When it returned to Coningsby it was also painted PRU–blue overall with RAF roundels and fin flashes. The RAF's first, and only, operational P-38 began marking operations immediately, Owen using it on the night of September 23 in a raid on Germany. It was used flown regularly on operations for a time, it is believed as a target marker and bomber controller, and was well liked by those who flew it. Eventually, when Air Cdre Sharp left for a new appointment his 'personal marker' went with him to Northolt. After the war it was flown into 51 MU at Lichfield for disposal, still in its unique RAF colours and was eventually returned to the US.

Text kindly provided by Andrew Thomas.

The only P-38 Lightning to fly operationally in RAF markings was 44-23517 which was the personal aircraft of the commander of No 54 Base at Coningsby. It was modified as a two-seater with a glazed nose. It never received a British serial number but carried the as yet unidentified code letters 'DPA'. *(J Rabbets)*

Fate of the Lightning Mk.Is in the US

Cl-26 : Class 26, aircraft withdrawn from use and stored. Some may have been used as instructional airframe afterwards and some may have been classified 26 after having DBR. It should be follow by an other RFC date but not shown in this case.
RFC : Refund Financial Center, or awaiting for scrap.

Total loss:

Date	Serial	Fate
12.01.42	**AE987**	Forced-landing, Seldfridge Fd (MI). 2nd Lt Charles Oackley.
	AF119	Nose wheel colapsed on landing at North Island (CA). Not repaired. 2nd William K. Walker
08.02.42	**AF115**	Loss of power on both engines and crashed, McClellan (CA). 2nd Lt Donald O. Starbuch.
22.03.42	**AE989**	Crashed on take-off, Paine Fd. 2nd Lt Robeert W. Neel.
	AF100	Forced-landing, Bradley Fd (CT). 2nd Fred J. Knauf.
06.04.42	**AF112**	Hit tree while flying low, Somerville. 2nd Lt Ray A. Keeney killed.
08.04.42	**AE982**	Crashed on take-off, Bradley Fd (CT).
16.02.43	**AF140**	Crashed 1 m W Moore Fld (TX). Maj Fred E. Hild.
30.03.43	**AF217**	Crashed near Casa Grande (AZ). Destroyed by Fire.
03.04.43	**AF156**	Flew into ground on TO, Rittenhouse Fld/Williams (AZ). AvCad Ben G. Conrath killed.
07.04.43	**AF111**	Crashed on take-off, Williams Fd (AZ). AvCad Robert G. Stranley.
07.05.43	**AF141**	Crashed off Williams Fld (AZ). AvCad Raymond J. Cayman.
10.05.43	**AF136**	Caught fire in air and abandoned. Crashed 5 m SE Chandler Fd (AZ). AvCad Herbert Brenner.
13.05.43	**AF142**	Crashed ¼ m E. Higley Fld (AL). P/O Basil E. Park (RAF).
04.06.43	**AF196**	Crash-landed, William Fd (AZ).
13.07.43	**AF209**	Crash-landed, William Fd (AZ).
16.07.43	**AF127**	Crash-landed, William Fd (AZ).
22.07.43	**AF154**	Crash-landed, William Fd (AZ).
23.07.43	**AF194**	Caught fire in air and CL, William Fd (AZ).
	AF210	Crash-landed, Wiilam Fd (AZ).
28.07.43	**AF177**	Belly landing, William Fd (AZ). DBF.
01.08.43	**AF139**	Forced-landing. 1 m NE Casa Grande (AZ). AvCad Russel W. Sly.
02.08.43	**AF190**	Forced-landing, William Fd (AZ). AvCad Olen M. Maxell
08.08.43	**AF172**	Belly landing, William Fd (AZ). Not repaired. AvCad John D. Lewis.
16.08.43	**AE999**	Crashed and burned 15 m. S Casa Grande (AZ).
26.08.43	**AF125**	Crashed and burned 1 m SE of Williams Fd (AZ).
30.08.43	**AF217**	Crashed, Casa Grande (AZ).
09.09.43	**AF209**	Crash-landing, Williams Fld (AZ).

P-322 AF207 while serving on a training base in the US. The armament has been removed as the P-322s were used as advanced trainers. AF207 was withdrawn from use in July 1943.

Withdrawal dates

AE978	Cl-26/08.06.44	AF142	Cl-26/13.05.43	AF206	Cl-26/02.06.43
AE979	Cl-26/08.06.44	AF143	RFC 6-45	AF207	Cl-26/10.10.43
AE980	Cl-26/08.06.44	AF144	RFC 6-45	AF208	Cl-26/16.06.43
AE981	Cl-26/07.10.42	AF145	Cl-26/15.10.43	AF209	Cl-26/21.07.43
AE982	Cl-26/08.04.42	AF146	Cl-26/31.10.43	AF210	Cl-26/09.08.43
AE983	Unrecorded	AF147	Cl-26/31.05.43	AF211	RFC 4-45
AE984	Cl-26/20.03.42	AF148	Cl-26/09.03.43	AF212	Cl-26/09.11.44
AE985	Cl-26/18.08.42	AF149	Cl-26/09.05.44	AF213	RFC 5-45
AE986	Unrecorded	AF150	RFC 2-45	AF214	RFC 6-45
AE987	Cl-26/12.01.42	AF151	Cl-26/31.10.43	AF215	RFC 6-45
AE988	Unrecorded	AF152	Cl-26/07.04.44	AF216	Cl-26/08.05.44
AE989	Cl-26/22.03.42	AF153	RFC 5-45	AF217	Cl-26/02.09.43
AE990	Cl-26/25.09.42	AF154	Cl-26/09.09.43	AF218	Cl-26/21.07.44
AE991	Cl-26/11.09.42	AF155	Cl-26/07.09.44	AF219	RFC 6-45
AE992	Cl-26/25.11.42	AF156	Cl-26/10.04.43	AF220	Cl-26/13.02.43
AE993	Cl-26/18.08.42	AF157	Cl-26/10.10.43		
AE994	RFC 6-45	AF158	Cl-26/10.10.43		
AE995	Cl-26/07.04.44	AF159	RFC 6-45		
AE996	Cl-26/22.10.42	AF160	Cl-26/22.06.44		
AE997	Cl-26/07.04.44	AF161	Cl-26/29.02.44		
AE998	Cl-26/08.03.44	AF162	Cl-26/03.08.44		
AE999	Cl-26/16.08.43	AF163	Cl-26/06.07.43		
AF100	Cl-26/10.04.42	AF164	Cl-26/08.06.44		
AF101	RFC 4-45	AF165	Cl-26/09.08.44		
AF102	Cl-26/11.06.44	AF166	Cl-26/31.08.44		
AF103	RFC 5-45	AF167	Cl-26/08.06.44		
AF104	Cl-26/19.02.44	AF168	Cl-26/02.10.43		
AF105	8th AF in UK - cond.01.01.46	AF169	Cl-26/12.10.43		
AF106	8th AF in UK - cond. 01.03.46	AF170	Cl-26/09.06.44		
AF107	Cl-26/07.04.44	AF171	Cl-26/16.12.43		
AF108	8th AF in UK - condem. 01.01.46	AF172	Cl-26/10.08.43		
AF109	Cl-26/08.10.42	AF173	Cl-26/15.06.43		
AF110	Cl-26/05.01.44	AF174	Cl-26/28.10.43		
AF111	Cl-26/07.04.43	AF175	RFC 6-45		
AF112	Cl-26/20.08.42	AF176	RFC 6-45		
AF113	Cl-26/25.06.43	AF177	Cl-26/29.07.43		
AF114	Cl-26/08.11.43	AF178	Cl-26/11.06.44		
AF115	Cl-26/18.03.42	AF179	Cl-26/08.06.44		
AF116	RFC 2-45	AF180	Cl-26/12.08.43		
AF117	RFC 6-45	AF181	Cl-26/08.06.44		
AF118	RFC 6-45	AF182	RFC 6-45		
AF119	Cl-26/31.08.42	AF183	Cl-26/21.06.44		
AF120	Cl-26/09.03.43	AF184	RFC 11-45		
AF121	RFC 5-45	AF185	Cl-26/22.07.44		
AF122	Cl-26/27.10.43	AF186	Cl-26/19.07.43		
AF123	RFC 5-45	AF187	Cl-26/18.03.44		
AF124	RFC 5-45	AF188	Cl-26/08.06.44		
AF125	Cl-26/29.08.43	AF189	Cl-26/28.04.43		
AF126	RFC 6-45	AF190	Cl-26/14.08.43		
AF127	Cl-26/21.07.43	AF191	RFC 6-45		
AF128	Cl-26/11.06.44	AF192	Cl-26/17.11.43		
AF129	Cl-26/26.06.43	AF193	Cl-26/26.06.43		
AF130	Cl-26/08.05.44	AF194	Cl-26/31.09.43		
AF131	Cl-26/15.06.43	AF195	Cl-26/01.12.43		
AF132	Cl-26/01.07.43	AF196	Cl-26/08.05.44		
AF133	Cl-26/06.09.44	AF197	RFC 4-45		
AF134	Cl-26/15.06.44	AF198	Cl-26/26.06.44		
AF135	Cl-26/15.06.44	AF199	RFC 4-45		
AF136	Cl-26/15.05.43	AF200	Cl-26/08.06.44		
AF137	Cl-26/08.06.44	AF201	Cl-26/17.02.44		
AF138	Cl-26/20.11.43	AF202	RFC 6-45		
AF139	Cl-26/02.08.43	AF203	Cl-26/08.05.44		
AF140	Cl-26/28.04.43	AF204	RFC 6-45		
AF141	Cl-26/13.05.43	AF205	Cl-26/18.09.44		

Cl-26 : Class 26, aircraft withdrawn from use and stored. Some may have been used as instructional airframe afterwards and some may have been classified 26 after having DBR. It should be follow by an other RFC date but not shown in this case.

RFC : Refund Financial Center, or awaiting for scrap.

With the RAAF

The RAAF did not use the Lightning fighter version. It only used the photo-reconnaissance versions which had the denomination of F-4/F-5 in the USAAF inventory. With the French and the Chinese, the Australians were the only foreign countries to use the F-4/F-5 in operations during the war.

After the fall of Singapore in 1942, the RAAF was looking for aircraft and the more modern, the better. These needs were somewhat fulfilled with the injection of Dutch materiel repatriated from the Dutch West Indies but these aircraft were already outdated. Also, on Australian territory, USAAF aircraft of various types found refuge having survived the first weeks of fighting. This disparate reinforcement would help the RAAF until new aircraft were available. Some modern aircraft, however, did make it into RAAF hands. Among these were a handful of Lockheed F-4-1-LO Lightnings. Three of these aircraft were used between August 1942 and August 1944 by No. 1 Photographic Reconnaissance Unit (PRU). The PRU had been formed in June 1942 with the aim to carry out long-range strategic and tactical reconnaissance flights at high altitude with a large variety of aircraft types. The first OC appointed to command the unit was S/L Lloyd W. Law.

The F-4s were part of the first batch of 99 machines and a derivative of the P-38E. They had four K-17 cameras to replace the armament located in the nose and were equipped with an autopilot to make long missions comfortable. After being stored at No. 1 Air Depot for two months, the first two F-4s were issued to No. 1 PRU on 31 October 1942. These were **A55-1** (ex 41-2158) and **A55-2** (ex 41-2159) and had been in service with the USAAF since January 1942. These aircraft had been painted in the standard RAAF colours of dark brown and foliage green for top surfaces and sky for the undersurface. No tactical codes were painted and none were carried during their long career with the RAAF. The introduction of these reconnaissance aircraft took place at the right time as the Japanese were trying to consolidate their position in the islands to the north and east of Australia. They were building airfields and facilities for invasion troops so it was crucial to know more about their activities. For this task, the Lightnings were based, south of Darwin, at Coomalie.

The first operational flight was carried out, above the Tanimbar Islands, on 3 November by Flight Lieutenant Bill Talberg. Six other flights were flown before the first accident occurred on 20 November. That day, Flight Lieutenant Alan Cridland suffered an engine failure in A55-2, while carrying out an engine test, and decided to land at Livingstone (Northern Territory). As he began his approach, he pushed the

Above, A55-1 while in service with No. 1 PRU (RAAF). The unit was based at Coomalie Creek.
Below, the same aircraft after a gale blew it into a drainage ditch on 11 January 1944. No codes were used on the F-4s.
(AHM of WA)

throttle forward and made a turn. The turn was too steep, he stalled and crashed four kilometres from the airfield, killing the pilot. To replace this loss the RAAF took charge of a third F-4-1-LO (its identity remains uncertain) in February 1943 that became **A55-3**. The transfer was organised directly with the Fifth Air Force. Arriving at No. 1 PRU after modifications on 16 March, A55-3 made its first operational flight on 21 March and both it and A55-1 were very active over the region in the following weeks (fifteen flights for A55-1 and nine more for A55-3 until the end of May and twelve for both aircraft in June). During a reconnaissance mission on 13 June, F/L P.B. Sinnott discovered the Japanese were building a long runway of 1800m on Selaru Island. Seven flights were recorded by the unit (now under the command of S/L Charles C. Lawrie) in July with three more in August. Apart from those reconnaissance flights, No. 1 PRU was also tasked by the Americans from time to time to take photographs of the targets bombed by the B-24s based at Darwin. During the following summer, the two aircraft were grounded to undertake 240 hours overhauls. Generally speaking, the serviceability of these aircraft remained low until their withdrawal. In February 1943, for example, only twelve hours' flying were flown. The best month was May with 65 hours.

However, despite the rather small number of flights, both aircraft would meet a tragic fate. Indeed, A55-3 continued its reconnaissance flights until 10 December 1943 when it was heavily damaged on landing at Batchelor (Northern Territory). The pilot, F/L Philip B. Sinnott escaped injury. The aircraft was sent to No. 4 Repair and Salvage Unit and was finally declared uneconomic to repair after 362 hours flown. Regarding A55-1, it was a one of a kind for most of 1944. After a non-flying accident on 10 January, it was kept far from the unit for subsequent repairs. Returning to 1 PRU in mid-August 1944, it was lost on the following 1 September when the undercarriage collapsed on landing at Coomalie Creek after returning from a test flight. It caught fire almost instantly and the pilot, F/L Carl J. Rush, was badly burned on the arms and part of his body. The aircraft was completely destroyed by fire. By that time, the Mosquito, a far more efficient and effective aircraft in the reconnaissance role than the Lightning, had been introduced into service with 1 PRU. The unit became No. 87 Photo Reconnaissance Squadron on 9 September.

In addition to the F-4s used by 1 PRU, a handful of loaned F-4s were operated by No. 75 Squadron based in New Guinea. This loan took place in 1943. Two are identified as being F-4 42-2220 (coded "20") and F-4 41-2156 (coded "56" and christened "Leaping Lizzie"). They were delivered to the squadron, on 16 August 1943, by Squadron Leader Geoffrey Atherton and Flight Lieutenant Brown who, with two other pilots, completed an accelerated course on the type at Port Moresby. These aircraft were tasked with providing reconnaissance flights under No. 9 Operational Group. Between August and December 1943 they carried out regular flights over the Markham Valley, Gasmata, Kiriwina, Goodenough Island and Cape Gloucester. Atherton completed 33 flights and experienced at least two. Three other F-4s were also allotted to the RAAF by the Fifth Air Force in February 1944 (41-2130, 41-2139 and 41-2217). All were eventually rejected in May 1944 due to their poor condition and also because the RAAF no longer had a need for the F-4 as the Mosquito had been selected for the role.

The F-4 coded "20" used by No. 75 Squadron RAAF, seen on Turnbull Strip (Milne Bay) while on loan from the 8th PRS of the 5th AF. *(AHM of WA)*

Summary of the aircraft lost on Operations - 1 PRU (RAAF)

Date	Pilot	S/N	Origin	Serial	Code	Fate
10.12.43	F/L Philip B. **SINNOTT**	Aus. 250837	RAAF	**A55-3**	-	-

Total: 1

Summary of the aircraft lost by accident - 1 PRU (RAAF)

Date	Pilot	S/N	Origin	Serial	Code	Fate
20.11.42	F/L Alan T. Cridland	Aus. 260424	RAAF	A55-2	-	†
02.09.44	F/L Carl J. Rush	Aus. 413433	RAAF	A55-1	-	Inj.

Total: 2

Above, A55-1 seen burning after its crash. Its pilot escaped alive but injured. *(AHM of WA)*

Left, the remains of A55-2 in which F/L Cridland was killed. *(AHM of WA)*

A55-3 of 1 PRU in flight in 1943. Generally speaking the F-4 was not always popular with American pilots and the USAAF chose on many occasions to use the Mosquito, and even the Spitfire, to do the job (especially in Europe). (AHM of WA)

THE REPUBLIC LANCER

The Republic P-43 Lancer was a development of the P-35 and the development of the P-43 eventually brought forth the P-47 Thunderbolt. The P-43 was built in small numbers, less than 300, and only one fighter group was fully equipped with the type in the US. The bulk of the production was ordered initially, under the Lend-Lease Act, as the P-43A-1 for British use but was soon redirected to the Chinese before the British allocated any serials. The P43A-1s were delivered between December 1941 and March 1942 but the contract was repossessed by the US when they entered the war. About 108 of them were earmarked for China with the Americans keeping about eighteen for their own use and modified as a tactical reconnaissance aircraft. Indeed, the USAAF, being short of tactical reconnaissance aircraft at the time, modified several aircraft types to carry cameras. For the P-43 it was in the rear fuselage. Only six of the US aircraft were modified to become P-43Ds while the modified Lend-Lease aircraft were designated P-43Bs.

The P-43 was introduced into RAAF inventory, like the F-4 and P-39, when the Australians were desperately looking for aircraft. At that time, some Lancers were available, either from the USAAF as the F-4 Lightning was becoming available in numbers or from the batch earmarked for China. Of the first source, these were four of the P-43Ds mentioned above and received the serials **A56-1, 2, 5 and 8** (41-6692, 6707, 6718 and 6685 respectively). Four B models were also delivered with the serials **A56-3, 4, 5 and 6** (41-31495, 31497, 31494 and 31500). The newly arrived aircraft belonged to a batch of six P-43Ds and an unspecified number of P-43Bs that had been shipped to the Pacific in mid-1942 for possible use by the Americans as a short-range tactical reconnaissance aircraft (something that never happened). In all, the RAAF took delivery of eight P-43 Lancers. Australia and China would become the only countries to use the type on operations.

The RAAF received its first Lancers on 31 August 1942 when four P-43Bs and two P-43Ds were delivered to No. 1 Aircraft Depot, at RAAF Laverton, Victoria. These aircraft had left the United States just over a month previously and had only just arrived in Australia in crates. Two further P-43Ds (41-6718 & 41-6685) were issued from USAAF stocks during the second week of November 1942 and became A56-7 and A56-8 respectively. These two had been shipped out with the previously mentioned six but it seems that they were briefly used by an unidentified Fifth Air Force Unit for evaluation and possible use in the region.

The aircraft were first tested and modified to RAAF standard with the four ex-P43Ds later receiving wing pylons to carry a locally manufactured 30-gallon tank or 250-lb bomb (the RAAF had thought to use the aircraft as a fighter-bomber but this idea soon reached a dead end). Five were issued to No. 1 PRU, formed the previous June, in mid-September 1942 and the sixth (A56-6) was held in reserve for future allocation. They were welcomed by the PRU as an alternative to their Brewster Buffalos.

The career of the Lancer was plagued with brake problems that led to several accidents. Here, A56-5 is seen after its accident on 14 December 1942. Like all the other aircraft of 1 PRU, no codes were carried. (*AHM of WA*)

On 26 November 1942, three P-43Bs (A56-3, 4 and 5) were sent to the forward echelon of 1 PRU at Hughes Strip. This was to be the first deployment of the type. One of the aircraft (A56-4) flown by F/O Bond was delayed because of brake problem. This issue would continue to plague the type throughout its service. In November the type flew 23 hours, more or less a quarter of the unit's total. In December brakes continued to give trouble and were the cause of an accident when A56-5, flown by Flight Lieutenant A.M. Angwin, crashed into the edge of the runway. The aircraft was sent for repairs along with A56-4 (still with brake problems) and, by the end of the month, only A56-3 remained serviceable. This was only for a short time, however, as its turbo-charger began giving trouble and the aircraft was unserviceable from 3 January onwards. A56-4 returned to the unit in mid-January but the problem with the brakes was not totally resolved and, by the end of January, neither of the two remaining Lancers were available. Few hours were flown that month but some local reconnaissance flights were carried out before the technical problems grounded the Lancers for the rest of the month. In February, things returned back to normal and the Lancers flew close to 30 hours, one third of the total hours flown by the unit, but no operational flights were undertaken. On 11 March A56-3 became unserviceable following an accident due to brake failure and left A56-4 as the only Lancer on strength for the rest of the month. Consequently only 16.5 hours were flown on the type that month and only three local reconnaissance flights carried out on the 27th, 29th and 30th to photograph various fields in the area. A56-4 continued to be the only active Lancer in April and completed about six local reconnaissance flights that month for a total of 21 hours of flight. Recurrent problems with the brake system, and the resulting poor serviceability, led to the withdrawal of the type from the PRU. A56-4 was sent away for storage on 16 May and A56-3, still under repairs at No. 14 ARD but officially on 1 PRU strength, never returned to the unit. In all, with the fifteen hours flown by the sole Lancer of the PRU in the final weeks, the type would have flown only about 100 hours over close to six months. The last official flight for the unit took place on 12 May when F/L Robillard was sent to photograph Fenton Field. The Lancer was unable to replace the Buffalo which was kept in service for a little while longer.

As for the aircraft issued to the PRU, but not sent to the forward echelon, things were not any better. A56-1, still unmodified at 1 AD Laverton, taxied into Avro Anson AW963 of No. 67 Squadron RAAF and was damaged on 25 March 143. The aircraft, piloted by P/O A.W. Green was taxiing out for take-off. Worse, on 29 April 1943, A56-7 was posted missing while on a ferry flight to Laverton where it was to become part of the Station Flight. It crashed in thick forest on the side of Gordon Gully near Healesville in Victoria but was not discovered until 1958. The pilot was again P/O A.W. Green. With no regret, all of the aircraft were returned to the Fifth Air Force between June and November 1943.

Summary of the aircraft lost by accident - 1 PRU (RAAF)

Date	Pilot	S/N	Origin	Serial	Code	Fate
09.12.42	P/O John E. **Macleod**	Aus. 416591	RAAF	**A56-6***	-	-
29.04.43	P/O Alan W. **Green**	Aus. 413433	RAAF	**A56-7**	-	†
	*on loan to 1 APU					

Total: 2

A56-6 was used for bomb carriage trials at No. 1 Aircraft Performance Unit at Laverton, and was damaged severely on landing at Laverton on the 9th December 1942, injuring the pilot, P/O J.E. Macleod of 1 PRU. The pilot unlocked his tail wheel and on application of brakes, the aircraft ground-looped to starboard. A56-6 was converted to components in March 1943.
(AHM of WA)

THE VULTEE VANGUARD

The Vultee Vanguard was a fighter offered for export by Vultee. As it was powered with a 1,200-hp engine, the USAAC and the USN showed little interest in the aircraft as 2,000-hp engines were under development. It made its first flight on 8 September 1939 and the program was able to go ahead when Sweden placed an order for 144 examples designated as the 49C in Vultee nomenclature. The production prototype flew in September 1940 and, after various tests, the rest of the order was built between October 1941 and April 1942. By that time the Swedish order had been embargoed by the US administration in an attempt to provide a quick response to the invasion of Western Europe by Germany in the spring of 1940. Indeed, the French had an urgent need of aircraft and asked for more Curtiss H-75s (P-36 in US nomenclature), between 150-200 airframes, but these could not be spared so the Swedish aircraft were seized instead. France collapsed in June 1940, however, before any aircraft could be delivered and the order was therefore earmarked for the UK and the serials **BW208-BW351** were allocated. The British intended to use the aircraft as an advanced fighter trainer with 72 on strength in Canada and the rest being taken on RAF charge. However, plans had changed, when the first aircraft were beginning to come off the production line in October 1941, and the entire order was taken over by the Americans under a Lend-Lease contract to supply the Chinese (with the denomination of P-66 and serials 42-6833-6975). The first four Vanguards (maybe more) were delivered with full RAF camouflage and markings before these changes took place.

Two views of the second Vanguard Mk.I built, BW209. They were built at Downey, in California.

†

IN MEMORIAM

Airacobra, Goblin, Lancer, Ligthning

Name	Service No	Rank	Age	Origin	Date	Serial
Bryant, Robert Murray	Can./ R.65736	Sgt	27	RCAF	23.07.41	336
Cridland, Alan Thomas	Aus. 260424	S/L	34	RAAF	20.11.42	A55-2
Green, Alan William	Aus. 406393	P/O	25	RAAF	29.04.43	A56-7
Hewitt, Peter Norman	RAF No. 101025	P/O	19	RAF	1910.41	AH582
Nette, Herbert Charles	Aus. 400728	F/O	28	RAAF	26.10.42	A53-5
McDonnell, Angus John	RAF No. 101020	P/O	19	RAF	13.02.42	AH602
Sawyer, Roy Ernest Frederick	Aus. 403113	Sgt	24	RAAF	13.12.41	AH581

Total: 7

Australia: 4, Canada: 1, United Kingdom: 2

A Airacobra taken during a test flight.

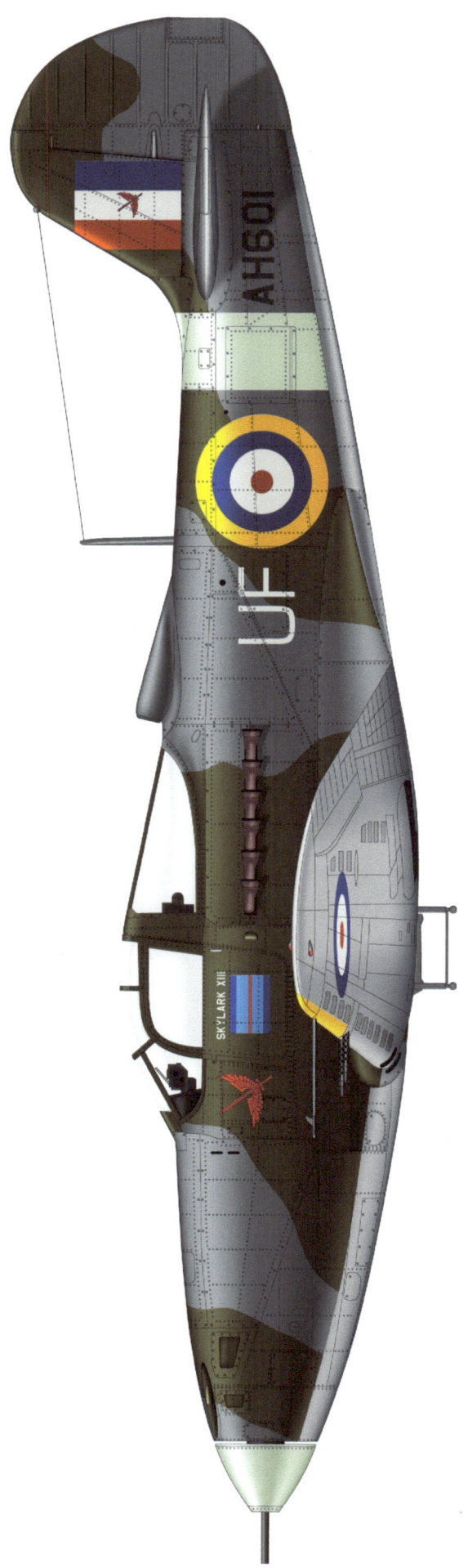

Bell Airacobra Mk. I AH601
No.601 (County of London) Squadron
Squadron Leader Edward J. GRACIE
Duxford (UK), October 1941

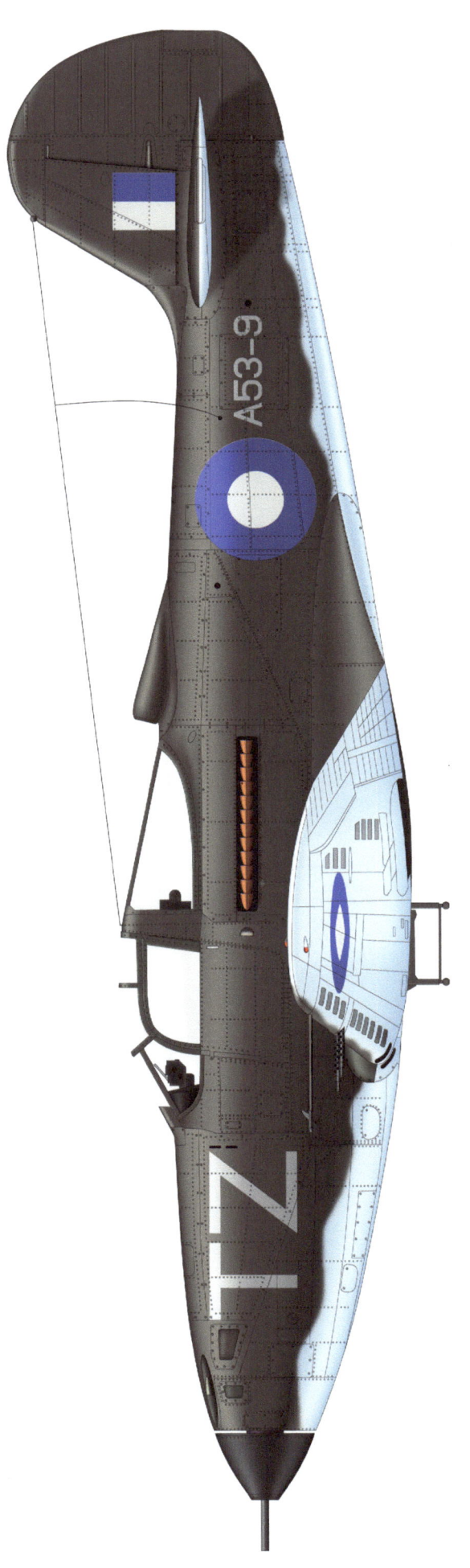

Bell P-39D-BE Airacobra A53-9
No. 23 Squadron, RAAF
Lowood (Australia), Autumn 1942

Grumman G-23 Goblin 344
No. 118 (Fighter) Squadron, RCAF
Dartmouth (Canada), Summer 1941

SQUADRONS! - The series

1. The Supermarine Spitfire Mk VI
2. The Republic Thunderbolt Mk I
3. The Supermarine Spitfire Mk V in the Far East
4. The Boeing Fortress Mk I
5. The Supermarine Spitfire Mk XII
6. The Supermarine Spitfire Mk VII
7. The Supermarine Spitfire F. 21
8. The Handley Page Halifax Mk I
9. The Forgotten Fighters
10. The NA Mustang IV in Western Europe
11. The NA Mustang IV over the Balkans and Italy
12. The Supermarine Spitfire Mk XVI - *The British*
13. The Martin Marauder Mk I
14. The Supermarine Spitfire Mk VIII in the Southwest Pacific - *The British*
15. The Gloster Meteor F.I & F.III
16. The NA Mitchell - *The Dutch, Poles and French*
17. The Curtiss Mohawk
18. The Curtiss Kittyhawk Mk II
19. The Boulton Paul Defiant - *day and night fighter*
20. The Supermarine Spitfire Mk VIII in the Southwest Pacific - *The Australians*
21. The Boeing Fortress Mk II & Mk III
22. The Douglas Boston and Havoc - *The Australians*
23. The Republic Thunderbolt Mk II
24. The Douglas Boston and Havoc - *Night fighters*
25. The Supermarine Spitfire Mk V - *The Eagles*
26. The Hawker Hurricane - *The Canadians*
27. The Supermarine Spitfire Mk V - *The 'Bombay' squadrons*
28. The Consolidated Liberator - *The Australians*
29. The Supermarine Spitfire Mk XVI - *The Dominions*
30. The Supermarine Spitfire Mk V - *The Belgian and Dutch squadrons*
31. The Supermarine Spitfire Mk V - *The New-Zealanders*
32. The Supermarine Spitfire Mk V - *The Norwegians*
33. The Brewster Buffalo
34. The Supermarine Spitfire Mk II - *The Foreign squadrons*
35. The Martin Marauder Mk II
36. The Supermarine Spitfire Mk V - *The Special Reserve squadrons*
37. The Supermarine Spitfire Mk XIV - *The Belgian and Dutch squadrons*
38. The Supermarine Spitfire Mk II - *The Rhodesian, Dominion & Eagle squadrons*
39. The Douglas Boston and Havoc - *Intruders*
40. The North American Mustang Mk III over Italy and the Balkans (Pt-1)
41. The Bristol Brigand
42. The Supermarine Spitfire Mk V - *The Australians*
43. The Hawker Typhoon - *The Rhodesian squadrons*
44. The Supermarine Spitfire F.22 & F.24
45. The Supermarine Spitfire Mk IX - *The Belgian and Dutch squadrons*
46. The North American & CAC Mustang - *The RAAF*
47. The Westland Whirlwind
48. The Supermarine Spitfire Mk XIV - *The British squadrons*
49. The Supermarine Spitfire Mk I - *The beginning (the Auxiliary squadrons)*
50. The Hawker Tempest Mk V - *The New Zealanders*
51. The Last of the Long-Range Biplane Flying Boats
52. The Supermarine Spitfire Mk IX - *The Former Canadian Homefront squadrons*
53. The Hawker Hurricane Mk I & Mk II - *The Eagle squadrons*
54. The Hawker biplane fighters
55. The Supermarine Spitfire Mk IX - *The Auxiliary squadrons*
56. The Hawker Typhoon - *The Canadian squadrons*
57. The Douglas SBD - *New Zealand and France*
58. The Forgotten Patrol Seaplanes
59. The Dutch Fighter Squadrons - *Nos. 322 & 120 (NEI) Squadrons*
60. The Supermarine Spitfire - *The Australian Squadrons in Western Europe and the Med*
61. The Belgian Fighter Squadrons - *Nos. 349 & 350 Squadrons*
62. The Supermarine Spitfire Mk I - *The beginning (the Regular squadrons)*
63. The Hawker Typhoon - *The 'Fellowship of the Bellows' squadrons*
64. The North American Mustang Mk I & Mk II
65. The Eagle Squadrons *Nos. 71, 121 & 133 Squadrons*
66. The Handley Page Hampden *Torpedo-bomber*
67. The North American Mustang Mk III over Italy and the Balkans (Pt-2)
68. The Hawker Tempest Mk V - *The expansion*
69. The NA Mitchell - *The RAF in the Far East, the NEIAF and the RAAF*
70. The Supermarine Spitfire Mk XVI - *The definitive operational history 1944-1945*
71. The Curtiss Kittyhawk - *The Canadians*
72. The New Zealand day fighter squadrons in Europe - *Nos 485 & 486 Squadrons*
73. The Supermarine Spitfire Mk XIV - *The definitive operational history 1944-1945*
74. The Hawker Typhoon - *No 609 (West Riding) Squadron and the 'Belgian Flight'*